AN EXHALATION OF DEAD THINGS

SAVANNAH SLONE

PRAISE FOR SAVANNAH SLONE

In a world quick to paper over its cracks and rot, AN EXHALATION OF DEAD THINGS stands in stark contrast, boldly and courageously balancing the beautiful, the abject, and the knowledge that everyone on earth will someday decay and disappear into the grinning void. These poems bring to mind Joseph Campbell's sage words of advice: 'the cave you fear to enter holds the treasure you seek.' Take a read and enter that cave!

FRANKIE SHAW, DIRECTOR, SCREENWRITER, ACTOR

An Exhalation of Dead Things, is an unflinching portrayal of identity and survival. These poems embody a constant state of becoming that is tied to the death and rebirth of self. Through intricate and piercing language, Savannah Slone confronts what is both personal and pivotal—moments that shape who we are despite what we have lost. An *Exhalation of Dead Things* will challenge readers to contemplate their various selves to ultimately become 'flowers from rust'.

DENISE NICHOLE ANDREWS, EDITOR-IN-CHIEF OF *THE HELLEBORE PRESS*

Each poem in Savannah Slone's *An Exhalation of Dead Things* feels like its own world, with its own nature and religion and laws. And in each new world, the speaker must adapt, must perform multiple "interstellar / breakdowns of Self" in order to survive. This is a book that reimagines and defamiliarizes the human form. Reading *An Exhalation of Dead Things* feels like watching a John Carpenter movie through your fingers.

PAIGE LEWIS, AUTHOR OF *SPACE STRUCK*

This new collection by Savannah Slone speaks of loss, identity, and grief; of love and bones and bodies; of 'ruined histories' and 'private pathologies.' *An Exhalation of Dead Things* is a deeply felt and exquisitely crafted work. Sit with these poems, breathe them in, for they are aimed and necessary and unforgettable.

KATHY FISH, AUTHOR OF *WILD LIFE: COLLECTED WORKS FROM 2003-2018*

With incandescent language and an unflinching honesty, *An Exhalation of Dead Things* performs an excavation of the self's existence in the body and the body's existence in the world. In these poems, we see the self as its 'misplaced fragments': unlit sparklers, trap doors, blank canvases. But just as a blank canvas nonetheless holds the promise of art, so too do these poems by the electric power of their language promise that through excavation one can find if not resolution then understanding, a laying bare of all that is longing, the 'science of urgency' with which the self moves through the world.

EMMA BOLDEN, AUTHOR OF *HOUSE IS AN ENIGMA*

CL◀SH

For survivors. For us.

CONTENTS

AN EXHALATION OF DEAD THINGS

PART I

neurotransmitters & other altered elements

COLLECTIBLES / COMMOTION

open my old trunk, find my trinket ruins
fish for vintage brushstrokes
find that confession is a church
is a cosmic captive

here are my handfuls of stars
this is an eruption
these are my telescopes for eyes
my dust drenched fingertips

this is my buried conservation
this is my shape shifting commentary
my galaxies of gaps, my private pathology
my worn quilts, my worn breaths
my accordion lungs, my indifferent mechanics

see the shade of concealer I wore was called *cadaver*
witness my quarantined attachments
feel my swarming thrusts
wade through my limp bones

DECAY / DETAIN

worship gnaws at my swollen throat
i dig through recycled jukebox songs
fingernails at my veins
powering my marionette arms
pressed flowers
weaved into my palms
my ugly, inverse,
inscribing a musk I can conjure
a possession, a primal hunger
an erasure of a vanishing
ribboning me out of wounds, hollow ridges
pendulums for eyes, halted in molding
pinned, framed wings
my desire in resin
i unveil my own decomposition

IMBALANCE, A REVOLUTION

vacant pockets
equating tin to
slender narrows
memorizing motions
adorned in
yellow linen
fermented sweat
where something calling
itself God slips in
a disobedient magic
a fevered writhing
a monument
a surgical repossession
an expanse   `chaos   matter
strike my strategies
struggling against thirst
flushed flesh
illuminated collapsings
clotted roots
my reflection, chewed up

                              spat

DISPROPORTION

fetal flood, pulpy teeth
lungs blooming mites
accumulating claustrophobia
viral fuel, erasing,
claiming my fossils like bullets
solitary, a blade:
conversations with
dead birds. intimacy,
a raging quiver
a religion
a movement
sketching my outskirts
outlining my bodily
shadows in the dark
jars of little mysteries
flecks of worn clasps
replicating burials
deconstructing
my motto song
humming through poison

swallows
satisfying my thirst
I am contaminated
I am unsullied

MISFIRING

cut paper dolls
with unsteady wrists
from my opal skin

your quivering slices an elegy
welcome our imperfect shapes to
the sea of two dimensionals

this is what it's like to own hips that slice
to have freckles in places only those who've
loved you know about

this is what it's like to be renamed after
every place you've called home, after
every person you've called home

this is what it's like to glow
this is a drained pool
this is one snaking streak of tail lights
this is an orange balloon, slipping out of your clammy grip

this is how you sprout flowers from rust
this is a paper cut
this is precision

WILT / TRIM

we are a conditional genesis   choking on our own morbidity

you watch me

                    reupholster our shapeless fingerprints

unveiling our brittle tongues   germinating the moss atop our threaded bones

cluttered wounds   pathological collapse   cradled candles

              sacred gravity, an offering

our after is a party   a weathered exhibition   a conclusive magic   a plum flame

          a window myth   our history, textured

severed subtlety   dislocated formalities   diversion   mess

we are reupholstered wounds   we unveil our shapeless tongues, our sacred

party   weathered   severed history   conditional bones conclusive   —   our mess, an after: a textured magic

an orbiting origin

WE, AN INSINUATED HUM

we, a collective
biopic, a dissolvable
blue, thawed
tongues
blur / eulogy / sleepwalking teeth
flightless transcriptions
carnage, conspiring
medicinal lunacy
a bleak worship
a moth chewed ellipses
filmy throats, biting deep
we, untethered
submerged in double
edged lust
framed episiotomies
molecular punctuation
a mystic alignment
a chaos that glows
a naked reverence
an eventual aftertaste

BREAK ME / MEND ME

this is an ode to
my misplaced fragments

an evidence, a promised

suspend me in still air

appraise my mercurial interiors
open me up, dog ear my pages
inhale my neon pink glow, my

intricate disintegration

confiscate my licked wounds
unbutton my oval mirrors
a fishnet chaos
human trash, a habit

rehabilitation enigma
an isolated copout
reflexive lacerations

a foaming absence

you, a straddled malady.

me, a rattled creature:
a stray altar
an uninhabited property

RESIN

i am my own trapped blood,
decaying in apology,
feral peach pits for eyes,
palms tucked into filled pockets—
fingering their hemmed
planetarium insides

i am a flashlit trash heap,
wading in a swell of crumbs,
a fog of untethered organs

i am the anti-inflammatories
i can't take. i am my
sweat stains, hoarse song sung,
eyes welded shut, tea clink

i worship the memory of
the fruitless rattlesnake strike

i am my own

clouded echoes being
drummer out after

SYNAPTIC PLASTICITY

my house is made up of pollinated apologies, rage collages, conjured mirrors, blood orange lips coming undone, dust clusterings erupt, the ghosts of swatted flies salt my melting cells, this is how we line the walkway, this is how we face one another, poppies and buttercups embroidered onto my velvet adhesions, stretched pulses lining the sea, lusting after the overflow, our pornographic vulgarities stare back at us. my house's floors are sticky with spoonfuls of tongued honey drizzling on my toes, i pry moths from window screens, my spilling guts descend the steps, my unsprouted seeds a bouquet, already withering, this is how we turn around, this is how we walk single file, back inside.

SUSPENSION

mourning a self-mapped anatomy is overdosing
on chronology, is the boney thick of ordinary

sharp inhalations are scratched glass
wildflowers lodged, an external lining

this mountain road, a spiral staircase
encased in fog, thirsting for flares

calculated lungs—incoherent pulsings
each day a new ruined history

i dig up sacrificial forget-me-nots
praying at the stems of the vanished

enshrining a discomfort
i can't disentangle

COUNTER CLOCKWISE

can you hear the quiet
shades of blue, the queued
hum, the conversational
bruises?

feel my belly
full of collectibles see my spoon
reflections tongue my swollen   clotty gums
see my marbled

face, my shattered
hereditary, my unlit
sparklers for veins, my inward
twisting nothing, hear my hands

scrubbing plates   assembling
furniture stroking you
awake

fingering stained
mugs clean hear the phantom
floorboard creak that is me that is my
periodic obsession   to become   something else

CYCLICAL WOUND

I don't trust honey that pours
I teach my dad slang
I harvest my own velvet organs
I am a pickled threshold
a half blown balloon, tied off
a beaten peach aftermath, a tiny
yellow house's electrical hum
a kaleidoscope trapped in a jar
I am a trap door   ajar
I don't believe in god, but I
feel left out of religions with exclusivity
I am a mess of misunderstood psychology
I am a Pac Man, aimlessly swallowing pills
I like to tell stories   I like
dodging follow up questions
I am a collective we with no friends
I am a pharmacy I am a bitter sip
I am a six-year-old
in somebody else's bathtub
at a party, alone

carving her bald legs
up with a lavender disposable razor and she
doesn't know the slices sting until her mom's
face tells her she's in pain.

REKINDLE

I build little homes for myself
in shadow lit hammocks
& reclined passenger seats
& the pube-ridden bathroom floor
home my soft body home
my harsh edged personality
home my sticky mango hands
my radiant asymmetry my
cranberry stained panties
my dead bolted orifices my sinking
furniture my melted off
fingerprints my bouquet of flowers I bought
pre-dead my shrill waves my
inherited triggers my crass glow
I build little homes for myself each day
all the while knowing I'll
never not be an arsonist

AND I'LL TELL YOU HOW IT FEELS

Saddle me with the regenerated
crossbreeds of your lusts and furies.

Blow
shotgun smoke
into my raw throat.

Drip water on my drying watercolor.

I am a blank canvas—
not ready for creation, but
manually choosing vacancy.

I am a vessel of empty prayers
of the nameless faces of your past.

I am the unbought—
the not yet purchased,
up for grabs,
littered erosion.

Adorn me in your abhorrence and
your favorite perfume.

Pin me down and tell me everything
I'm not. Draw my portrait and craft a grin
out of my timeworn face.

Now, tell me how I feel and I'll tell you how it feels.

TO LATE NIGHT APPREHENSIONS

swallowing smoke through the whistle ruins
uncaged bird skeletons catch fire
furnace bones a memorial of cologne stench
dissolving hospitality
taking flight with phantom wings
that you dreamed up, but forgot to check on.
iron alignment
aching for a shift
pianos keys' mouths sewn shut
only threaded murmurs that no one can piece together
cello body, rotting sternums
covered in dust
plucking at your inner workings
fingering your shape shifting,
esophageal disassembly of grey,
speckled eggs
that you can't identify
you rub fern underbellies on stinging nettle leg
sky murky from weightless body
malleable marine surface from the great below

turning pages, newspaper flinch
hostile arms that can't wade
your verbal sorcery latches cage
door shut.

MY ARCHAEOLOGY

chapped lips filled in with red felt pen

velvet aftermath left behind

self portrait shadow print a pixelated

unofficial baptism

oozing fissure a crevice of sacrificial solace

translucent human suit crackle with vapor

trying to stay afloat

a transient on the sidewalk of my own story

staggering on fractured stilts back to the epicenter of my flowering casket

old lace chrysalis

womb revisited

AN ODE TO MY HEART

My beating vessel, my weeping ukulele pump, stripped down to moss on bark. You can rip my heart from its cavity—I don't need it. Just give me my own personal full moon and I'll tie a rope around it: a lantern for my night-time trepidations. The muscular cadence of my anxieties that could kill—leaving you perspiring, trespassing; yes, you're an intruder now. But I left my door unlocked and you didn't know you were stumbling into a live wire, sparking with that mystic mythical spark that they talk about. Pulling you into the chamber of the beneath. You carve out your heart and sew it into my chest and I need it, even though I don't.

THE ANATOMY OF MY MEMORIES

my little pasts live in
my elbows
my lilting eyelids
my shape shifting mole
my phalangeal joints I fracture with pleasure

my circulating sockets
my bruised, synthetic knees
my handfuls of hips

my raw throat
the hinges of my retracting mouth
in the lines of my fingertips
the etched trails of my palms
in the liquid synapses of my marionette mind

when I start to forget, I take a swig and my mechanical bones remember

LITTLE JOYS

clanking metal
hip bones
we gauge
one another's
latitudes
and longitudes
mercurial
echoes of fingertip
metronomes
moss ablaze
emerald and auburn
cornea reflections
less birds, more bees
honeysuckle filth
mortal mythology
a premature
stinger prick

LITTLE HURTS

littered glass
shards of humanity
mimicking a wishbone tug
pulling the trigger on god
suicide of the sky—the Out There
an assembly of the disassembled hollow
sprouting alignment—fevered womb

A WRINKLE IN GRIEF

whitewater rafting in molten silence,
a blunt abstraction
to distract yourself from your own humming of
insufficient hymns
melancholy was served as an appetizer
with a dirty glass later filled with water
with mostly melted ice cubes
that day
and it didn't matter
because how could anything matter
when you're mending your soul
lacerations with patches of anointed amnesia
sewn tight with silver seams but the
light still invades through the slits
since you're not very good at sewing
wounds, your flux repairs an attempt worth giving up on

WRITINGS ON THE WALL

She steps on the heads up pennies in
the grocery store parking lot. She walks
under ladders, chasing black cats that
cross her path to tell them that they are important
and worthy and everything she needs to hear. She strokes
her plum rabbit foot keychain after each family tragedy.
She applies thick black smudges of dull eyeliner with the
help of a shattered pocket mirror that still gets the job done.
You say knock on wood and she doesn't move a muscle.
You say fingers crossed and her open palms
caress her own body, disobeying your destiny.
Willing your misfortune as if she were rerouting the lines
on your palms, tampering with your tarot stack.
She walks to a hip hop headphone beat and enters the elevator,
umbrella still ajar. She presses the button for Floor 13
and you drop
dead.

PART TWO

on claustrophobia

ETHEREAL JUNCTURES

morbid reverence a blurred
funeral where hushed shrieks muting the sheathed
build up inside as the neglected
areas of my subconscious
fight their way out through the spaces in between the thread
I needle into my eyelids
trying not to see
when blindfolds aren't enough anymore
stitches fall unfastened
my mind's bleakest corners
resurrected as my nocturnal hysteria sets in
hostile recollections unmasked
ethereal juncture, carved
deep into my fossil bones
clanking together as I
walk whispering our own unspoken language back to me
even when I cover my ears
I thought I moved on until I
saw my own body:
a graveyard.

THE EVOLUTION OF ENORMITY

unfocused black and white checkered floor seen
through poor eyesight: spectacles long lost
you see her, Mother, cut through sunflower stems with rusty scissors her ocean of
hair sways daringly in the manmade breeze of the cheap rotating fan
in the bedroom, you apply bark for wallpaper
life, for you, a Monet painting

peach acrylic paint singes
into your nostrils
abandoned car idles, driver's door ajar, in a vacant
snowstorm
aroma of gas and metal,
snow covers bloodstains of the ones who presented you

a single cupcake lit by a match (it took three attempted matches before one would take)
scratch pad abrasions make you itch all over
a silent birthday song sung by a room of tongueless nobodies
mouths smack, but no words come out
you blow out your single candle, a gust

that disrupts the hush: room, fades to black

cactus makes skewers
of your blueberry stained fingertips
Mother lays upside
down, adorned in violet lace that hugs, on a velvet armchair
her hair caresses the hardwood floors that you carved
around her numb body

you paint a whale on the seafoam
brick wall and smile a orange-red lipstick teeth-stained smile
that tastes like the crayons you weren't supposed to eat as a kid
dusty moth flaps wings in slow-motion on your tongue
single cupcake baked with salt instead of sugar
she licks her thorn pricked finger and you can taste it, too

LIMINAL EDGINGS

of evolved contraception.

You: a contraption of memorization, waves of permission.

An illuminated
antique of what Infatuation
should
be.

Our stories don't exist in time zones,
floral printed tool belts
carry all the baggage we allow ourselves to display:

Different Flavors of Fucked Up.

Our embroidered eyebrows
house erotic winks and tears that
decay and natural disasters that deconstruct lives.
They oversee
what you do and did.

LOVING HER

pale moonlight blooms on the hardwood
floor of the home I call
us
me, a honeybee, over-saturated, drowning
in a sea of suppression, liberated by the gentle
hands of you, my beekeeper
humming in tune to one another's deep,
endlessly celebratory breaths
the vinyl spin of your mermaid song,
chicory tucked tight into your mane
shaking hands with myself for the first time,
unveiled my eyes to self
saying goodbye to the bottled-up pariah
when the weight seems to wilt—
fading into the void
that I'll never swim back to.

THE SLOW DOWN

I still know my small self well:
faded yellow one piece
slow mo juvenile canter through sprinklers
fade to black and white
faded
indiscernible with sun mutilation
but your rose quartz eyes
guide me on.

Borders of dandelion root
contain matte memories:
depression disbelief,
you leave me
leaves in my lattes
cheek kisses both nettle and sage.

Rosemary scented embrace as
Van Morisson's "Moondance"
plays and we slow dance as
I sear the margins,

stroking your
pearls for nipples,
your textbook areolas—

You: a fortress to my wasteland.

YOUR HONEYCOMB / MY INNER CHEEK

cast little spells of salt on my rusty moth bones / my inner cheek crimson,
honeycomb treating my thrush / I melt into the underneath, my vocal
chords your vaccine / my chattering rag doll jaw a spreadsheet of the space
between your temples / skin stained green by empty antiques / explosion of
scabs, a lost game of operation / a dimmed scrape at oblivion / crack your
joints and I'll fall to the ground

LUNAR

I long for a cosmological relocation a lavender planet a marmalade dream a blackberry compote where humans plant ferns and poppies and poison ivy where men hear "no"

where snakes pulse around your wrists crystal constellations rose quartz galaxies bodies of water—bodies of life.

A planet whose moons are prayed to by the visionaries and the creators and the ones who question where microscopic languages heal scars, solstice deposits, hidden in drawers, never go deprived.

We: undiscovered.

Where the moons rise and we rise, too.

THE (SELF) LOVER: A TAROT CARD

You've drawn this card because you're likely at a crossroads. A fork in the road.

Catch-22.

No lovers need apply.

The (Self) Lover indicates your need for that primordial connection

that self-intimacy that out of body balance held within, your fragile focus a quandary.

Draw again.

Now, shuffle.

ORIGINS OF THE HOLLOW

fleshy bird
wings blot
out fog
ocean spits
out iridescent
fish, pumping
out waves
of silence,
plastic bags
moonbathe
A civilization
of radiation:
woven crucifixion—
origins of
the hollow.

AN EXHALATION OF DEAD THINGS

I could write a how to guide on breaking
I have a celestial allegiance to all of my seared transgressions
and breaches, violations, infringements
                and   breakings
of the molten women I've been
the pronouns I've lost and found
                    the masks I've tried on
all extraterrestrial identities broken,
off to the landfill of my subconscious, no time for braking,

I hem a moonscape for all of my selves that I'll be
and have been
and am
and will dream about within my
        interstellar
                breakdowns of Self.

GESTAT(I)NG

tinfoil crown
fistfuls of belly
fever sprout
blister sliver
rusted sutures
suspending
her maternal
marionette body

ultrasound jelly
clasps onto
her ramparts
a liquescent
phantom blanket
draped
dancing womb
silhouettes
on the blank walls

the geography
of my mental

furniture
a blurred,
abandoned
incantation
of a home
that once was

peony contracts
signed with molten
blots
sealed with wax
a spool of human
parts dissolved
by thread cutter
hemming you a feast

Immaculate Rejection

foraged
clinging
ashes
scattered vowels
a blushing
wound
a collection
of crimson petals
the thirst
of mortality
tattooed
on my forced
open palm
marking me
into the After

MY BODY IS A HOUSE

and you are my front door

    your eyes on me are my blindless, naked windows

        your caressing palms, my door knobs

            I am a vessel of bitter losses and findings

                my body is a house, but yours is a home

PEWTER AND PEBBLE

birds coast in configurations out the window,
reflections on your laptop screen. hypnotic ribcage

heaves.

Coming Out is putting everything on the line:
an orphic sinkhole, knowing life will undoubtedly alter.

unveiling
your inner workings,
your sinkhole of self
bearing your narcotic
teeth as you bite
into that ripe
peach
and warm honey oozes
out, dribbling
down your prickly
chin—
neck and hands
        and thoughts
left immobile with adhesive.

guzzling down that effervescent elixir seeking an assemblage of catharsis,
left only wilting as your tinny voice sounds.

sharing that bumblebee
hum of words that shouldn't have to be said.

the world goes pigeon grey for just a moment.

SMALL

Mouse brown
mushroom haircut.

Navy blue tie-dye spaghetti strap top.

Having tea with bears
on white wicker   tiny furniture.

My favorite friend, a plush and rubber
monkey in a tuxedo,
gamey grin, a banana
                              welded
into his palm.

My bears' sewn on mouths
mirroring apathy.
Monkey's perpetual smile
made me remember how
I had to seem, too. Mouth tacked upright
under small eyes, under
a haircut I'd remember.

EXTINGUISH ME WITH UNLEADED

artifice child plays
barber knifes my scalp
dripping wound floods
my inner ward   abandoned
nerve endings light
flares on the side of the road

that is   closed   on   both   sides
seamless humanity plates shift

overlapping
          over
                    me: the weeds in the cracks

landlocked, I confess, but still I am shackled aflame

BRED

blurred crevice
chalk screech
transluscent caesarian
shave 'em, prep 'em
cul de sac bones
disinfectant illusion
economic residue
involuntary forceps
materialized stirrups
earthy sear
moist pucker
intravenous arm-twisting
depreciating sequel

WE ARE A HOUSE FIRE

trickle your egg white ooze
down my honey throat
blow your helium breath
into my budding balloons
swell me with your contraband
gut me with your barbed jaw
take small bites out of my redwood core
reach the dead end as I rot
my roots eager thighs ajar
your fingers tiny arsonists

MAGIC, BLUE LIGHTS, AND VELVET
LOVESEATS

missed peripheral grasps
kick me in the stomach. I can feel
my own palm as if it weren't my
own. like rubbing cream colored
silk against cream colored silk.
foreign slow motion
walking meditations with you, all in my head.
your northern lights firefly eyes glow
a surgeon's glove blue.
Resuscitation.
deep breaths feel like orgasms
when I'm drunk on perception.
slow pedestrians
slow clap
and we move slowly, too.

A PROPERTY OF COEXISTING BONES

visceral rookie
>virginal concoction

duffeling up monogamy
>bent spoons clanging in their respective

homes in the unevenly
>never-quite-closed drawer

>molding anonymous clay

a property of coexisting bones
>weightless telescope creatures

pacing down
>mouthfuls of not-yet-named streets

passing by flaggers
>cones

caution tape
>lingering in the lukewarm cyanide

>pool that is human traffic

peddling against our own geographies
>topographers of our own pasts and nows

intimate cyborgs
>migrating magnets

facing the wrong ways
          in the shadow quiet
hour of the night.

BATH TIME

turn the tassel of the cloudy faucet
season water with salts
lilac nail polish
plum cheekbone(s)
scalp sweat
lukewarm myths
molten eyeliner drip
historic clavicles

water so hot you see the heat on the horizon
you half-expect a cowboy to walk up
a cowboy who can walk on water
a cowboy Jesus

rest your forehead on your bent knees
two doors half shut
taste the salt of yourself
belly rolls
mismatched areolas
dry   prickly knees

gaze through the window of your thighs

see your hands
dancing coyly
flirting
pointer fingers inching together
your very own Creation of Adam

massage yourself clean
making your bath milky

cracking joints sounds different underwater

lay back, everything underwater but your nose

                                                                eyes

                                                                       nipples

            now, float.

UNCOVER MY HOLLOW

unveil my tethered roots:

                                        outskirts

unzip my heavy molar
my watercolor waves
my pale ribcage

deflower my inlaid scapula
stitched with thick wool
thinning thrusts aflame
accelerating tonsils, heaving melody

because my quilted uvula has depth
a patchwork profundity
thoughtfully placing tree seeds that are   grown   like   me
standing tall in the dusty moon radiation
            intersection inquisition
match strike

PART THREE

marionette choreography

MECHANICAL HORTI(CULT)URE

show me the ghosts
you hide in the gaps
between your teeth.

offer me your rusty shovel
let me bury myself
alive in the iridescent
webbing of your flaccid
throat. bile inhalations,
I won't mind.

for my birthday,
I'd like to peel away your
scarring. gift me your human
suit, my Automaton.

shrink me down to size:
entomb me
in your sliced away umbilical cord.
or did your mother swallow it whole?

be the punch line to my illusion.

sprout flowers from your scalpel
lesion, thank me, thank me very much,
when they're plucked
from your garden

placed on your headstone.

FIELD NOTES ON BECOMING YOURSELF

pluck fallopian
foxgloves from your diseased roots

egg trek   cardiac harvest

wear insects as rings,
arthropod legs caging each digit

around your neck, trilobites

rusty toenails
scratch off achilles blisters

stack blocks with your beet stained gums

pick suckers from your armpits
swallow them whole:
      deer ticks,   your aphrodisiac
palpitate your inner

embryo with your lidded palms

hush the textile secrets of your eyes' backsides
chlorophyll impregnations, a souvenir

sway to the comfrey
swallowing bee hum

translating itchy veins
a lost   now   Found treasure

opal smoke out your lapel felt cuckoo clock,
your urn

titanium gears for joints
revolving as you try on mannerisms

morphed curiosity
you, a novelty

embroidered bullet hole
cello beak,
stitched shut

VENAL EXODUS

Chalkboard paint. Bruises.

The Midnight Cousin
Hallway Attack "horsing around"
kind of bruises. Cigarette exhalation wafts

seep into pores. Three sizzling ticks, pulled

loose from juvenile, hairless armpits.
Chewing tobacco forearm
application: bee stinger

liberation. Water sprinklers the only

drink the hay for grass will be seeing.
Butt burnt by rooftop sun glare.
Warm wind blows book

pages the wrong direction.

I give up.

I go in.
Two swift snaps. Caught

"playing sex" in Grandma's Powder Room.

Eyes that pierce, perforate. Snap. Snap.
The slow-motion heart
beat as we can't do anything

and the police don't do anything

and then one curt shotgun blast
heard through the phone. Bang.
Mom's boyfriend stains field

crimson with self-inflicted farewell.

Phone drops, hovers. Cord bounces it
as it levitates in limbo. Humming shrieks
ooze from levitating phone. Now:

fall face first into the couch. Real

sex in Grandma's Powder Room. Fast,
fast forward. Child drives, child
graduates high school, child

births child. Child takes child

to school. Innocence drowned.
Innocence envied. Chalk screeches
stiff line. Bruises fade. Cigarettes
tamped into ash. Armpits sliced

by shaking shaver. Snap. Snap. Bang.

Are you still crying because he did this to your family or are you just mad
that now you won't
ever get to take
This option
out?

UNADORNED

Lick me with your warm
honey tongue. Give me your port-wine
stain birthmark.

You are your pale
moonlit clavicles,
clanking against mine.

Pencil erasers for nipples.

You are your blue
painted toenails and your bare
hands and your silver
nose hoop and your chipped
tooth. You are your ear
piercings that you wear unadorned,
filled back in with scar tissue.

You are your black tattoos.
Bottle you up for me: sweat and

lavender and
chalkboard paint. A labyrinth
of stretch marks, belly button
encircled: iridescent tree rings.

You are your subliminal reach for me in the night

AT NIGHT, SHE TAKES OUT THE TRASH

it is that hour of the night
when the mud of my leftovers sing
out to me. her flat tongue is against
my carotid artery against
the counter when I smell it. over there.   overfilled.
avocado smoke. groceries, the forgotten, the intentions, the cupidity. the lingerings
fruit fly eruption. sullied diapers.
freckled banana peel drop. wrung out, worn
earl gray tea bags. my own little landfill. the mud
of my leftovers. my strawberry

ooze. ginger-tipped q-tips. holding my
nose like an amateur swimmer. staggered
dance through the lamp lit mess of the day,
yellow drawstrings digging into the lines of my palms

dog eager for the outside, following close, longing for escape
and me too
I dodge the spider web, the garden orb weaver
moon is a streetlight is the moon

dense noise of breath. mosquito bite. tin can clang. owl's neck swivels. shadow passerby.
amphibian hum. river static
return to an accidental marinara splash   a missed toss of a red bell pepper
 that I don't scoop out, that I don't wipe up
white bag retrieval   tuck
and I don't look back
it is that hour of the night when

I am not mommy or lover

I am just a thing with shit that I conceal with the unsoiled

MOLDING THE PULSE

our reveals aren't pink and blue
it's a human we cry and we cry
because we can   we can
mold the pulse of
self-consuming self
hands intertwined snakes
camouflaged in rose folds
a pieced together glow
our ribs and joints, little midnight snacks
we keep everybody else well fed
our malleable opens and closes trespass
their vapor borders
into the throbbing
pores of the property
of us: we, their astringent

we are characters who survive
who don't have to come out
our past, a parody ailment

we cultivate waves of human buzz
our selves are not legalities
we are less birds and more bees
we don't wear black to the cemetery
no longer an other, but an us
thrusting headfirst
with hunger.

THIS BODY IS MY OWN

my permission slips are tucked away neatly
you can ask and I can say no and you can listen
I can strip down I can paint
thick streaks of acrylic over your eyes
I can unmask your ears to tell you something
rip the duct tape from your mouth because your body is yours, too
and I can listen
you can ask and trace the single line sketch of my outer self

they didn't, though, and I'd turn to stone,
I'd wade into the tide pool of the underneath

this body stained limbs, ripe
ready for plucking, begging not to be plucked
these magical eye bags, heavy lidded bridges
broken blood vessels

they made this body a crypt in the shade
they gifted me gravel knees
that body a complying ribbon
this body an off kilter button

that doesn't want your alterations

my innards are impenetrable roots

they don't see the twists and turns of my body's roads
they don't see the speed limit signs
they're the self-appointed law enforcement
this body's stop signs, driven over

this body is an alchemist   my gold, your leftovers

but my surveillance cameras have eyes

this body is my own
my permission slips are tucked away neatly
you can ask and I can say no and you can listen

this body is my own   and you will listen

THIS IS THE BENEATH

These are our eyes that can't blink.
These are our chipped teeth.

Our luminous, opal
buttonholes that we sew
together. Me, a marble ghost,
gazing into the mirror that isn't
really there.

This is my sea of hips.
Ilium.   Ischium.   Pubis.
This is you, jangling my little
pieces together like keys.
I sleep in a dissolving trundle
bed that doubles as an operating
table.   I am a self-surgeon.

        This is the dissolving inaudible.

My tendons, even my cuticles, are in recovery.
This body is a clinic.

This is a paper shredder,
where we lay within.
We, embers.
Them, tattered maps.
This is the prologue and
the epilogue.
                    This is our body.
Intramural plum cheekbone(s) pillars holding
me up.

WE, IN THE REAR VIEW MIRROR

the rear view mirror tree trunks,
rebirthed post-forest fire. the whale spout

eruption. backwards-facing
ball caps. protruding bills.

dressed in wildflowers. dandelion
cadavers ablaze. we are the herbivores

of the creeks. the rubbery bodies with masking
tape for joints. we are our

salty fingers. our   fistfuls of lye.

chastity belts fashioned
from thick lace.

rosemary palms, praying
hands' friction   sparks.

YIELDING YOUR RIPE FRUIT

take pungent compost in your palms
find it a home—moisten it, yeah, plant your seeds deep

conceal us, don't wait for a reaction.
each unsolicited thrust a stationary   tamp   tamp   tamp of the soil

put us in a warm space
give us water, oxygen,   grab us by the ponytail

yeah, your hands are filthy now
we are the ebony underneaths of your nails

our slow motion necks, forcibly nodding against the ground our eyes fixed,
glazed—jaws, merciful; loose fists

we, two colliding freight trains
one rampant, blind; one out of diesel, derailed: lights out

oil spills down tracks into garden
germinated transplants left choking on dirt

revolting out from the beneath. now, sow your greasy poppies
they bloodstained, limp. now, watch us

frown when they shrivel on the dining room table
the morning after, the in betweens of our legs still sore.

FASTEN AND UNFASTEN ME

and let me watch you do it.
this is my favorite buttonhole. I sewed it myself.
this is what was once a small rip
from that time I got caught on splintered wood

fasten and unfasten my inner mendings
these are my refractions

will you be my pallid cerulean on anesthetic nights?

I am my own agency, yes, this is what I make autonomy look like and these
are tiny lime green paint stains because sometimes I just don't think, isn't
that right?

place your palm on my anemic ribcage
do you feel that slow motion pulse of leaves?

these are my chipped nail polish extremities, my stained teeth, my chipped
tooth, my brass headboard, my rotting floorboards, my quilts, made with
love, my tainted quilt's, cigarette burnt by somebody else. these are my late
night benedictions, my slow blink over afternoon tea.

I want to be your micro macro.

I want to hyperventilate by your side, syncopated blackouts.

cavity collaboration: a collection of sharp edges and soft breaths.

let me be your astringent.

I can be your witch hazel, honey.

your obsidian worry stone.

your ticklish hip bones' very best friend.

let me unfasten you and you can fasten me back up, sew up the open spaces

I FILL MY OWN VIALS

caress me in the syllabic lamplight
our hollow peach pits for coronary cavities have skeletons on the inside
we have our own little lung languages

this is the electric blue of the smoky autumnal sun-up
this is my smile, note the bark for teeth
consider my paper trees for limbs
peel away my outer bits

this is the shift click we feel and know
across a room, our eyes shift click, we are
pop up characters in a fourth graders' diorama on what love looks like
or maybe sin

this is my pointer
this is my pie chart
these are our statistics

unravel me from my ribboned self
bare bent backs unzip
millipedes needle their way out

let me be your conditional coroner
I am your magnified radiation
you are my initiation,
my finch song, but

you, my phlebotomist,
you find my veins

CHECK MY VITAL SIGNS

with skipping stones and seaweed
trace the outlines of my mothered teeth, stained tea green

mountain laurel hypnotism
tomato rust splatter, dove oysters:

this is fog

thickening with molten permanence
bruised shins, my blood, metallic and thick

honey wax filling in the cracks in my molding,
blurred ballerina, upturned eyelids, dried fruit for skin

I am the mold stench
laundry sopping, forgotten,
I am the aftermath of putting myself last

a science experiment

disrobe my scalpel seared chest

an open casket
autopsy, check
an exploration of dust mites and garden orb weavers
morning dew on the grimy cages and wardrobes of my innards

I fill a mason jar with apple cider vinegar and dish soap
and the fruit flies fly on in through the holes I poked with care
with a dull secondhand knife, just like I wanted them to.

I go inside, too.

WE ARE OUR VERY OWN

fragmented window to the algid of the outward
not-yet-snowing stratosphere aftertaste,
that pallid cerulean of anesthetic nights,
lime green
lines of cheap
plastic alarm clocks
reading off those accidental
2s and 3s to us, again and
again, our eyes dry, probing through obsidian
our alarm cord—we, wall's off-kilter
outlet, we, florid's rounding of catacombs
we delect out the brindle
in us, we whet our exposeds.

TO ALL OF THE BOYS
WHO MADE ME SMALLER

you were there and then you weren't.

you weren't there, in the
pale bed sheet pallet aftermath,
my rotisserie neck
swallowing hard, in tandem
with the others I knew and did not.

I was not alone. I am not alone.
& that's a problem.

your uninvited words and touchings and hurts
all kinesthetic disembowelings of our
ribcage landscapes, a lagoon of
junebug hums and foggy irises.

you tightened your binocular grip,
looking into and past us,
we sweat through the maze of our cosmic palms

you salted our wounds and named it our remedy

you made us into small things of limbs
and hips
and molten quartz

and you are nothing

GUESSWORK

surveil me,   your curio

    your ripe appetite

    your circulating vulgarities

    your vulgarities: formulaic razorblades

quarantine breakings

    disarming collectivity

honeyed boil

    seared architecture

transcending echoes

    bellowed flexings

occupied foreshadows

    calloused suffocation

in-utero, enraged

    floating   worn

singeing my sculptings

    rewinding slices

gospel gust, gut

    me, drowning neighbor,

    my exodus

    my switchbacks for forearms

my unburied battlefields
my in betweens

my nowheres

DISMANTLE MY ODDITIES

with swelling bees, a swelling grip, a syllabic blink

activate my vessel belly with vinyl smog
watch me, detecting valves with a flowering tongue
swallowing the sealed off, vomiting
finality through my broken
vocabulary, quilting the skinned

embroidering cheekbones:
contaminated spasms of sunken
white hot, your sweat my nectar

succulents erupt from your tiny holes
I unplant poppies   rhythmic floor thump

our hard thrusting claps are cobalt
flickings of desire, our touch is made up of purple
light and sharp-edged shapes

and your wilted fingertips melt off of my hipbones
oily glow turned rot turned devour me turned devour me, please

you were just a thing
I could only solidify
before it was too late it's too late

THE UPSIDE OF THE PREDESTINED

mourning hinges   freckles of witness   floating ribs

a church for the suspended / a hospital for the bound

ghosts marrying sticky midnights   splinters bleeding me out lanterns

dissolving   overexposed contours

this is a symphony of absence and conjured language splintering

autonomy strumming tendons with my teeth indebted to vanishing

sacrificial passengers

celestial prescription pads   free-falling from basements

this is the song of the uninhabited, only fruit flies caught in a jar this is

what it sounds,

                              this is what it all sounds like

WE, LIMBLESS TREES

fluourishing chiselings
indebted to imminence, fire light
eye mirrorings, dulling sharpness
with sharpness, full moon, a thing
I can cup in my handsk
constellation memorials, wick
trimmed, lantern tip, oil fire
simulating urgency with unbridled mandibles
chewing up the steam you let off
these are my blacks and blues,
your golds and violets
elastic blood clots   sterile altars
glittering bruises, a coping mechanism
oiling the linen of my necktie
one thread away from decapitation   reflex violence
overdosing on trespassing ambiguous by proxy
christening the wallpaper with thick smoke
the thirst of multiplication
flesh, a sanctuary
smudging out the unsolicited

sucking in hard just to button my pants
shattered syntax, monologue breakings
the art of wait
pledging little licks   guttural transparency
touch yourself with my dislodged throat on your mind

INNATE

you make me want to learn all of the types of butterflies / you give me daydreams of insects / i needle blue thread through my puffy knee backsides / i gift you an abundance of singularities made up of the throbbing slow motion of our technicolor etchings / outlines of our crossing offs and counting downs / shadows of our intersections / nourishing our urns / tangling our little hurts / simulating confrontation / interchanging our opaque inheritances / covering each other's mouths / no, we were born without mouths / we are oozing mounds of skin, organs / we are glittered wirings / this is the science of urgency, a study on pendulum swings

MUZZLED MAGIC

First: open door. Descend porch steps. Key, ignition. Enter real world. Leave comfort of your home and hear the anthropoid clamor that never dims. Then: The melodrama of peripheral euthanasia, yarn scrapes against cracked palms. Playground of ghost tongues, hyperfixate over the hills of your body as you clang out slang and mumble grief, hungry for nostalgia and vinyl and the naked wooden montage of your moonless eyes that don't see me. My blue hair stains my shirt's shoulders in the rain, you don't stop talking. You don't stop talking about nothing. Now: exit / ignition / ascend / deadbolt / mute / recharge. / Haunting dissolutions of velvet fog treetop quilt, manifestation condolences and other forgotten, fossilized teeth. Scattered mouths pulse in the graveyard of muzzled magic

PART FOUR

an unveiling

HOLLOW LUNGS, EYES, KAZOOS, AND FINGERNAILS

We bury disassembled
rag dolls, pouring the nectar of humanity
over top the neglected
handcuffs.
Our mystical wild
eyes flutter
among the discarded
crayons. We see the dark-eyed,
deafening earth
swallow the cheap feathers—
drawn down in the black glass,
among hazy
footprints of blood.
These faceless footprints
render our shattered
tongues outnumbered.
Our crooked mouths duct
taped. Our jaws gripped
by the vibrating
fingernails of our nemesis.
We see the delicate peach pits

in the urns of your overall
pockets. We hear your
shadow. The watercolor
humming of the bees
and their kazoos make us swallow
the florescent Morse code rot
of our minds' inner workings. Inky cigarette
ashes shiver
beneath the graffiti
rot while conceptualized universes
dance in the machine shadows.
You discard empty
prayers of empty generosity.
They shimmer from your gold,
hollow lungs.

THE SUM OF HER PARTS

chew up the grit of my anatomy
find gravity in my coins for eyes
clench my skin, inflate my hunger
slow blinking petals for skin
hard swallowing wounds abloom
sprouting underarms
my flowering axed skull
budding mammary glands
take root, my kneeling cervix
hungry hymens
spoon feed my orifice
now tend to your flowering anus

BURY US ALIVE

our lungs still beating
pave over our transparent
roots, our opaque
inheritances, our
sheltering unsanctuaries

you pronounce our names wrong

your tongue flicking
backwards, tripping over
itself, you rewinding
VHS player, you

we climb elastic fences
we are the inevitable
moles, earth worms,
other small creatures
that find their way
back to the surface

we are the slow motion

plurals, the widowed
virgins, the whores of your
dreams, we are the red
thread at your grandmother's hem

we are the christened aftermath
the conjured bodies
we are the housewives
hiding the knives
oil that slips through your grip
that you can never quite unfeel.

FORESHADOWING THE PAST

webbed ribcages
stringy inhalations
clammy hinges
chiseled cellulite
shadow   glow   chrysalis
underexposed hum
churned out mothers
hollow splinters finding
their way out
ghost perfume
homes for orphaned bumblebees
in betweens
honeycomb organs
stacked sticky throat
horizontal fingertip circles
calloused into carpet
stagnant reaction
ripe with sin
every breath in,
a violation

SCULPT ME, I'M YOURS

malleable, ready: wear me in   dismantle my scraps
slice   peel
disarm me
give me insides
their own sense
of architecture
singe me with direction
reroute my cosmos
activate my little winces
buff out my surfaces
be my midwife, be my
embalmer
build my tongue up
with your own
hold your breath
while I flex
bow your head   say amen   light a candle   fuck me in mantras
when you have me
where you want me

then melt me back to nothing

TAKE SMALL BITES

widows wear weeds,
they wear peach
painted trilobites for
fingernails, black lace
panties sliced neatly,
against hardy hip
bones, with antique
shears, their sage
bunches lit aflame,
smoldering wafts. deep
crimson liquid lipstick,
spread with steady
hands. spreading succulent

time lapse. forgotten
taupe feather pile,
heavy with dust,
at the base
of an iron cage.
left behind legless,
gripping feet. widows

wear the weeds
the unwed toss
in the compost pile.
wick blown—fade
to black

I CAN CONJURE MY OWN FLOWERS

I'm just a creature who hates the word *panties*. whose autopsy proclivities display imbalance, a dusty excavation. who says amen at all the wrong times. an injured fleck of hollowed gold. a forbidden lover. an anticipated presence. who will halt in submission out of, what some call, politeness. whose lingerie looks best folded, tucked away. who contracts autonomy through self-portraits painted after midnight. whose seams are rusting. whose cellulite is spreading. whose handwriting is hurried scratchings. whose under eyes are like attics, are like formations of tender hums. whose bound mutings are like mantras. who wants you to cremate me. who still wants a headstone.

ACKNOWLEDGMENTS

I am grateful to the editors of the following literary magazines who have previously published poems from this
manuscript.

And I'll Tell You How It Feels – Pidgeonholes

To Late Night Apprehensions – decomP magazinE

my archaeology – Rag Queen Periodical

An Ode to My Heart – Dirty Paws Poetry Review

The Anatomy of My Memories – Crab Creek Review, Semi-finalist for 2018 Crab Creek Review Poetry Prize

little joys – Rag Queen Periodical

little hurts – Rhythm & Bones Lit

A Wrinkle in Grief_ – Okay Donkey

Ethereal Junctures – Rag Queen Periodical

The Evolution of Enormity – decomP magazinE

liminal edgings – TERSE Journal

Loving Her – Francis House

Nocturnal Monster's Self-Care Routine – Rhythm & Bones Lit

The Slow Down – Pidgeonholes

Your Honeycomb / My Inner Cheek – FIVE:2:ONE #thesideshow

Lunar – Anti-Heroin Chic

An Exhalation of Dead Things – Anti-Heroin Chic

gestat(i)ng – YES Poetry

my body is a house – Rose Quartz Journal

Pewter and Pebble – Rhythm & Bones Lit

extinguish me with unleaded – 8 Poems Journal
bred – Thin Air

we are a house fire – Rose Quartz Journal

A Property of Coexisting Bones – formercactus
bath time – The Occulum

uncover my hollow – Rhythm & Bones Lit

mechanical horti(cult)ure – Glass Poetry Journal

Field Notes on Becoming Yourself – Thin Air
unadorned – Hobart Pulp

at night, she takes out the trash – Hobart Pulp

molding the pulse – Thin Air

this is the beneath – Moss

we, in the rear view mirror – Crab Fat Magazine

yielding your ripe fruit – You Are Not Your Rape Anthology

To All of the Boys Who Made Me Smaller – You Are Not Your Rape Anthology

I can conjure my own flowers – Pithead Chapel

hollow lungs, eyes, kazoos, and fingernails – Manastash Journal of Writing and Art

The following poems appeared in Savannah Slone's chapbook, Hearing the Underwater (Finishing Line Press, 2019): "Venal Exodus", "Cynicism and Other Synonyms", "magic, blue lights, and velvet loveseats", "hollow lungs, eyes, kazoos, and fingernails", and "Muzzled Magic".

ABOUT THE AUTHOR

Savannah Slone is a queer, bipolar, and disabled writer, editor, and English professor who currently dwells in the Pacific Northwest. She is the Editor-in-Chief of Homology Lit, as well as the author of Hearing the Underwater (Finishing Line Press, 2019)

ALSO BY CLASH BOOKS

LIFE OF THE PARTY

Tea Hacic-Vlahovic

THE ELVIS MACHINE

Kim Vodicka

TRY NOT TO THINK BAD THOUGHTS

Matthew Revert

FOGHORN LEGHORN

Big Bruiser Dope Boy

50 BARN POEMS

Zac Smith

NAKED

Joel Amat Güell

REGRET OR SOMETHING MORE ANIMAL

Heather Bell

ALL THE PLACES I WISH I DIED

Crystal Stone

THE SMALLEST OF BONES

Holly Lyn Walrath

WE PUT THE LIT IN LITERARY

CLASHBOOKS.COM

TWITTER

IG

FB

@clashbooks

Email

clashmediabooks@gmail.com

Publicity

McKenna Rose

clashbookspublicity@gmail.com

Printed in the USA
CPSIA information can be obtained
at www.ICGtesting.com
JSHW082355140824
68134JS00020B/2090

9 781944 866945